Jack and the Beanstalk

LEVEL 3

Retold by Coralyn Bradshaw
Series Editor: Melanie Williams

Pearson Education Limited
Pearson
KAO Two
KAO Park
Harlow
Essex
CM17 9NA

and Associated Companies throughout the world.

ISBN 9781292240084

First published by Librairie du Liban Publishers, 1996
This adaptation first published by
Penguin Books 2000
7 9 10 8
Text copyright © Pearson Education Limited 2000
Illustrations copyright ©1996 Librairie du Liban

Retold by Coralyn Bradshaw
Series Editor: Melanie Williams
Design by John Hawkins
Illustrated by Claire Mumford

Printed in China
SWTC/07

Published by Pearson Education Limited

For a complete list of titles available in the Pearson Story Readers series please write to your local Pearson Education office or contact:
Pearson, KAO Two, KAO Park, Harlow, Essex, CM17 9NA

Answers for the Activities in this book are published in the free Pearson English Story Readers Factsheet on the website, www.pearsonenglishreaders.com

Once upon a time there was a little boy.

His name was Jack and he lived with his mother in a small house in the forest.

They were very poor.

One day his mother said,
'We've got no money, Jack.

'Take the old black cow to
market and sell it.

'Buy some food with the money and be careful!'

4

The next day Jack met an old man on the road.

The man said:

'Your cow is old and ugly.

'Take my five beans and give me your cow!'

'Five beans

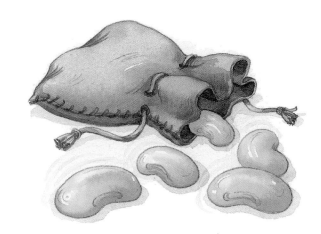

for my cow?

'Oh no! My mother will be angry.

'We've got no money and no food.

'I can't give you my cow for five beans,' said Jack.

'But they're magic beans,' said the old man.

Jack gave the cow to the man.

The man took the cow. Jack had magic beans
but he had no money and no cow.

His mother was very angry.

'Five beans for a cow!' she said.

'But mother, they're magic beans,' said Jack.

'Silly boy,' said Jack's mother and threw the beans outside.

The next day Jack opened his eyes and looked outside.

What a surprise!

In the garden he saw a big green beanstalk.

It went up and up and up!

'Ah! The magic beans,' said Jack.

He started to climb the beanstalk and climbed

quickly up and up and up to the sun and the clouds.

He was not afraid.

At last he came to the top and stopped.

'What a beautiful castle!' he said.

The sun was shining and it was hot.

Jack was tired and thirsty.

Jack went to the castle.

A woman opened the door but she was afraid.

'Be careful!' she said.

'My husband's a horrible giant and he likes to eat children.'

Suddenly the horrible giant came home.

'*Fee, Fi, Fo, Foy!* I can smell a little boy!

'Where is he?

'I want to eat him for my dinner!' he said.

'Quickly Jack! Jump into the bread oven,'
said the giant's wife.
'The giant will never find you there!'
Jack hid in the bread oven. He was not afraid.

'There's nobody here,' the woman said to the giant.

'Sit down and be quiet and eat your dinner.

'Look! A big plate of potatoes, peas, carrots and chickens.'

The giant ate all the food on the plate.

Soon he was tired and went to sleep.

Z-z-z-z-z-z.

Jack climbed out of the oven
and saw a bag of gold.

16

He took the bag and climbed quickly down the beanstalk.

He told his mother where he got the gold.

'Be careful! Don't go up the beanstalk again,' she said.

But the next day Jack climbed the beanstalk again.

Up, up, up to the clouds and the sun and the castle.

He was not afraid. He wanted more gold!

The woman gave Jack some bread and milk.

He was very hungry.

'Be careful!' said the woman.

'The giant is very angry because he can't find
his bag of gold.'

Suddenly the giant came home.

'*Fee, Fi, Fo, Foy!* I can smell a little boy!

'Where is he?'

Jack jumped into the bread oven again.

He listened to the giant.

'There's nobody here,' said the woman.

'Sit down and be quiet and eat your dinner.'

The giant ate all the food on his plate

and soon he went to sleep.

Z-z-z-z-z-z.

The giant had a magic hen.

Cluck, cluck, cluck....... a golden egg!

Quickly Jack climbed onto the table and took the hen.

He carried it home to his mother.

The next day Jack climbed up the beanstalk again.

The giant was angry.

'*Fee, Fi, Fo, Foy!*

'I can smell a little boy!

'Where is he?

'Where is he?'

Jack was in the bread oven.

He was not afraid.

The giant was tired and hungry.

He ate all the food on his plate and soon he went to sleep.

Z-z-z-z-z-z.

24

This time Jack took the giant's golden harp.

But the giant heard him and woke up.

'Stop, come back,' he said.

Jack was not afraid.

He ran very quickly.

The giant was very tired and very old and ran very slowly.

'Come back, come back!' he said.

But Jack ran to the beanstalk and climbed down quickly.

'Quickly mother, it's the giant, he's coming!

'The horrible giant is coming.

'Cut down the beanstalk.

'Oh quickly, quickly!' said Jack when he got to the bottom.

Jack's mother was very afraid but she was also very strong.

She took the axe and ran to the beanstalk.

'Oh dear, oh dear!' she said.

Jack and his mother quickly cut down the big beanstalk
with the axe.

Chop, chop, chop, chop.

Down, down fell the giant.

C-R-A-S-H.

That was the end of him!

Jack and his mother were very happy.

They had the bag of gold,

the magic hen

and the golden harp.

So they were rich and lived happily ever after.

Activities

Before you read

1. Look at page 8. How many beans can you see? What happens when you put beans in the garden?

2. Look at the picture on the front of the book. Where do you think the boy is going? What do you think is at the top? Tick (✔) the right picture:

After you read

1. Look again at activity 2 above. Were you right?

2. Match the picture with the right word:

axe, cow, castle, giant, harp

3. Look at the picture. It is not coloured in. You can colour it but be careful to match the numbers to the right colours.

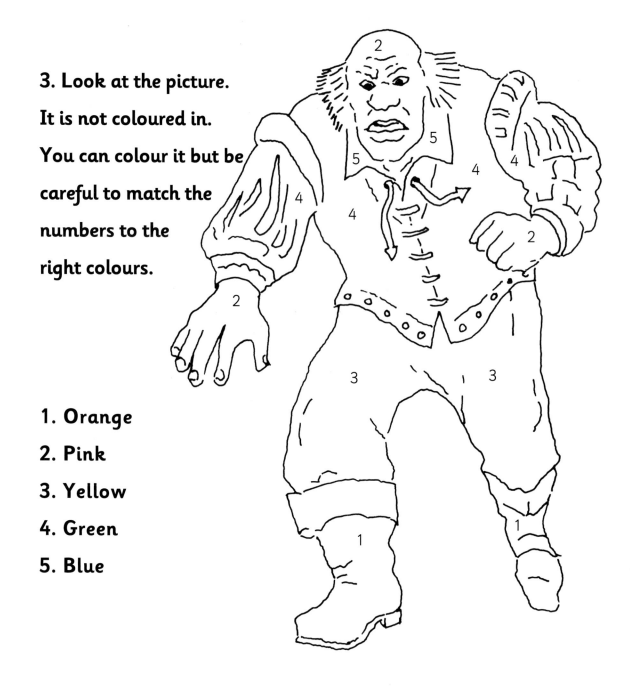

1. **Orange**
2. **Pink**
3. **Yellow**
4. **Green**
5. **Blue**

— — — — —

When you have finished, find the word in the story to match your picture. Write the word under the picture.

4. Either draw a picture of Jack and his mother at the end of the story:

Jack and his mother were very happy.

or draw a giant of your own.